Microsoft
Stream

The Microsoft 365 Companion Series

Dr. Patrick Jones

OLYMPUS ACADEMY
PRESS

TABLE OF CONTENTS

REDEFINING VIDEO COLLABORATION

In today's fast-paced, digital-first world, video has become a cornerstone of communication, learning, and collaboration. From training sessions to company updates, video allows us to connect, share, and engage like never before. But managing and organizing video content across teams and organizations can feel overwhelming—until you discover Microsoft Stream.

Microsoft Stream is more than just a video platform; it's a comprehensive tool for managing, sharing, and interacting with video content. Integrated seamlessly into the Microsoft 365 ecosystem, Stream empowers organizations to communicate visually, connect teams, and engage audiences with ease.

Video isn't just for marketing or social media anymore—it's become essential for businesses, educators, and individuals. Consider the ways video is already a part of your workday:

- A manager records a quick walkthrough of quarterly results to share with their team.

- An educator creates a series of tutorials for remote students.

- A team captures a brainstorming session to review ideas later.

Microsoft Stream makes all of these scenarios easier by providing a centralized platform where videos can be stored, organized, and accessed securely.

Example: Sarah, a training coordinator at a growing company, struggled with managing a library of onboarding videos. Using Stream, she was able to organize her content, make it searchable, and even track who viewed it—all within one platform.

What sets Stream apart from other video platforms is its seamless integration with Microsoft 365. It works effortlessly with tools like Teams, SharePoint, and OneDrive, creating a connected ecosystem that simplifies video sharing and collaboration.

Imagine recording a meeting in Microsoft Teams and having it automatically saved to Stream, where it's securely stored and easily accessible to your team. Or embedding a training video directly into a SharePoint site, complete with interactive features like captions and comments. With Stream, the possibilities for productivity and engagement are endless.

Whether you're new to Microsoft Stream or looking to enhance your video strategy, this book is your guide to mastering this powerful tool. Through clear explanations, practical examples, and actionable tips, you'll learn to:

- **Understand Stream's Features:** Discover how Stream fits into your workflow and its unique capabilities.

- **Leverage Integration:** Maximize productivity by connecting Stream with Teams, SharePoint, and more.

- **Engage Your Audience:** Use interactive features like comments, captions, and analytics to boost engagement.

- **Simplify Video Management:** Organize, store, and secure your video content effectively.

Sarah's Journey with Stream

As with the other books in the *Microsoft 365 Companion Series*, this guide follows Sarah, a relatable professional who learns to use Microsoft Stream to solve real-world challenges. Her journey—from overwhelmed training coordinator to confident video strategist—offers practical insights and inspiration for your own experience with Stream.

In the chapters to come, you'll explore everything from the basics of what Microsoft Stream is and why it's essential, to advanced topics like using AI-powered Copilot to create smarter workflows. Each chapter builds on the last, equipping you with the tools to transform the way you use video in your organization.

Whether you're a seasoned professional or just getting started, this book will help you unlock the full potential of Microsoft Stream. Let's begin this journey together, and discover how video can empower you to work smarter, connect deeper, and communicate better than ever before!

WHAT IS MICROSOFT STREAM?

Microsoft Stream is a video management and sharing platform that empowers individuals and organizations to create, organize, and distribute video content with ease. As part of the Microsoft 365 suite, Stream integrates seamlessly with tools like Teams, SharePoint, and OneDrive, providing a centralized hub for all your video needs.

Whether you're recording a training session, hosting a virtual event, or sharing updates with your team, Stream is designed to make video content accessible, secure, and interactive. It transforms how organizations communicate, learn, and collaborate by enabling users to harness the power of video effectively.

Microsoft Stream combines simplicity and sophistication, offering a range of features tailored to enhance productivity and engagement:

1. **Video Creation and Uploading**

   o Record videos directly or upload pre-recorded content.

   o Automatically save Teams meetings and webinars to Stream for easy access.

Example: Sarah used Stream to upload a series of onboarding videos for new employees, ensuring her team had a consistent and accessible resource.

2. **Organization and Search**

   o Use channels to group related videos, making them easy to find and manage.

   o Benefit from intelligent search powered by AI, which allows users to find specific moments in videos based on spoken words, captions, or keywords.

Pro Tip: Add tags to your videos to improve discoverability within your organization.

3. **Collaboration and Sharing**
   - Share videos securely with specific individuals, teams, or the entire organization.
   - Embed videos directly into Teams channels, SharePoint pages, or PowerPoint presentations for seamless integration.

Example: Sarah embedded training videos in her team's SharePoint site, providing a one-stop resource for her department.

4. **Engagement Features**
   - Enable comments and reactions on videos to foster interaction.
   - Use closed captions to make videos accessible to a diverse audience.

Pro Tip: Add quizzes or polls to your videos to create an interactive experience.

5. **Analytics and Insights**
   - Track views and engagement metrics to measure the impact of your content.
   - Identify popular videos or areas for improvement through detailed analytics.

Example: Sarah used Stream's analytics to monitor which training videos were most watched, helping her refine her content strategy.

One of Microsoft Stream's greatest strengths is its seamless integration with other Microsoft 365 tools:

- **Teams:** Automatically save meeting recordings to Stream and share them with participants.
- **SharePoint:** Embed videos in SharePoint pages for company announcements, training, or project updates.
- **OneDrive:** Store videos in OneDrive for Business and link them to Stream for wider distribution.
- **PowerPoint:** Insert Stream videos directly into presentations for impactful storytelling.

Pro Tip: Use Stream in combination with Teams and OneDrive to create a unified video workflow, where content is created, stored, and shared seamlessly.

Video is no longer just a supporting tool—it's a key driver of communication and learning. Microsoft Stream makes it easier for organizations to:

- **Enhance Communication:** Use video for company-wide announcements, ensuring messages are engaging and impactful.
- **Promote Learning:** Create a library of training videos and tutorials accessible to employees anytime, anywhere.
- **Boost Collaboration:** Capture and share brainstorming sessions, project updates, or team milestones.

Example: Sarah's company used Stream to host quarterly updates from the CEO, making the content accessible to remote employees who couldn't attend live meetings.

Microsoft Stream is a versatile tool designed to meet the needs of a wide range of users:

- **Business Teams:** Improve collaboration and streamline knowledge sharing.

- **Educators:** Deliver engaging lessons and tutorials for students.

- **HR Departments:** Standardize training processes and track onboarding progress.

- **Event Planners:** Record and share live events or webinars for broader reach.

Pro Tip: Use Stream to create a centralized video repository for your organization, ensuring all content is easily accessible and well-organized.

Unlike traditional video platforms, Microsoft Stream focuses on security, integration, and interactivity:

- **Enterprise-Grade Security:** Videos are protected within your Microsoft 365 environment, ensuring only authorized users can access them.

- **Interactive Features:** Closed captions, comments, and analytics make videos more engaging and accessible.

- **AI-Powered Capabilities:** Intelligent search and transcription features save time and improve the user experience.

Example: Sarah relied on Stream's transcription feature to quickly find specific moments in long training sessions, saving her team valuable time.

Microsoft Stream is more than just a video platform—it's a tool that enhances how teams communicate, collaborate, and grow.

WHY USE MICROSOFT STREAM?

In an era where video content dominates communication, training, and collaboration, Microsoft Stream offers a unique platform designed to make video management simple, secure, and impactful. From improving engagement within teams to enhancing learning opportunities across organizations, Stream's value lies in its ability to transform the way people interact with video.

This chapter explores why Microsoft Stream is an indispensable tool for businesses, educators, and individuals, highlighting its advantages and real-world applications that make it a standout choice in the Microsoft 365 ecosystem.

1. Centralized Video Management

Why It Matters:
Video content is only useful if it's easy to find and manage. Scattered video files across email, local drives, and cloud storage lead to inefficiency and frustration. Microsoft Stream solves this problem by providing a single, secure location to store and organize all your video content.

- **Streamline Organization:** Use channels to categorize videos by project, department, or topic.
- **Effortless Search:** Leverage AI-powered search capabilities to find specific moments or topics within videos.

Example: Sarah's HR team centralized their onboarding videos in Stream, ensuring new employees could access them at any time without searching through multiple platforms.

Pro Tip: Use Stream's tagging and metadata features to make your video library even easier to navigate.

2. Enhance Communication Across Teams

Why It Matters:
Video is one of the most engaging ways to communicate, but traditional methods like email attachments or links to external sites can be cumbersome. Stream's integration with Microsoft 365 enables seamless video sharing, enhancing communication within teams and organizations.

- **Simplify Updates:** Record announcements or updates and share them directly through Teams or SharePoint.
- **Boost Engagement:** Use video to convey complex ideas visually, reducing the need for lengthy text explanations.

Example: Sarah's marketing team recorded weekly updates and shared them in Stream, allowing remote members to stay informed without scheduling additional meetings.

Pro Tip: Embed Stream videos in Teams channels or SharePoint pages to make them easily accessible to your audience.

3. Foster Collaboration with Interactive Features

Why It Matters:
Collaboration thrives when everyone can engage with shared content. Microsoft Stream goes beyond passive viewing by allowing users to comment on videos, ask questions, and provide feedback.

- **Comments and Discussions:** Encourage team input and dialogue directly on videos.
- **Closed Captions:** Make videos accessible to all team members, including those with hearing impairments or language barriers.
- **Reactions:** Use likes or emojis to acknowledge ideas or contributions.

Example: During a brainstorming session, Sarah's team recorded their meeting and uploaded it to Stream. Team members later added comments and ideas directly to the video, enriching the discussion.

Pro Tip: Enable commenting on training videos to let employees ask follow-up questions or share insights.

4. Empower Learning and Development

Why It Matters:
Video is a powerful medium for training and education, and Microsoft Stream elevates it by making content engaging, accessible, and trackable.

- **Create a Training Hub:** Organize all your educational content into channels for easy access.
- **Track Engagement:** Use analytics to monitor which videos are being viewed and for how long.
- **Interactive Learning:** Add quizzes, polls, or knowledge checks to reinforce key concepts.

Example: Sarah's company created a library of compliance training videos in Stream. Employees could access the videos at their convenience, while managers tracked completion rates to ensure compliance.

Pro Tip: Combine Stream with Microsoft Forms to integrate quizzes directly into your videos.

5. Save Time with Seamless Integration

Why It Matters:
Switching between tools disrupts productivity. Stream's integration with Microsoft 365 ensures your video workflow is efficient and cohesive.

- **Teams Integration:** Automatically save meeting recordings to Stream for easy sharing and archiving.

- **SharePoint and OneDrive:** Store, organize, and share videos across your organization without duplicating efforts.

- **PowerPoint:** Embed Stream videos directly into presentations for impactful storytelling.

Example: Sarah's team embedded a product demo video into their PowerPoint pitch deck, providing a seamless and professional presentation.

Pro Tip: Use Power Automate to set up workflows, such as notifying team members when new videos are added to a Stream channel.

6. Maintain Security and Control

Why It Matters:
For organizations handling sensitive or proprietary content, security is critical. Microsoft Stream ensures your videos are protected within the secure Microsoft 365 environment.

- **Permissions Management:** Control who can view, edit, or share your videos.

- **Enterprise-Grade Security:** Protect content with advanced encryption and compliance features.

- **Privacy Options:** Choose between public, organization-wide, or private access settings.

Example: Sarah uploaded a confidential strategy session recording to Stream and restricted access to her management team, ensuring sensitive information stayed secure.

Pro Tip: Regularly review and update video permissions to maintain security.

7. Drive Engagement with Analytics

Why It Matters:
Understanding how your audience interacts with video content helps you refine your strategy and create more impactful content.

- **View Metrics:** Track the number of views and watch time for each video.

- **Identify Trends:** Determine which videos resonate most with your audience.

- **Refine Content:** Use insights to create more engaging and relevant videos.

Example: Sarah noticed that her team's product tutorial videos had low completion rates. She used analytics to identify where viewers dropped off and shortened future videos to maintain engagement.

Pro Tip: Use analytics to monitor whether training videos are being watched and adjust content or delivery as needed.

From enhancing communication to empowering learning and development, Microsoft Stream offers unparalleled value for individuals and organizations.

GETTING STARTED WITH MICROSOFT STREAM

Microsoft Stream is designed to be intuitive and accessible, making it easy for anyone to begin leveraging its powerful video management capabilities. Whether you're uploading your first video, organizing content for a team, or integrating Stream into your existing Microsoft 365 workflow, this chapter will guide you through the essentials of getting started.

Step 1: Accessing Microsoft Stream

Stream is part of the Microsoft 365 suite, so if you already have a subscription, you're just a few clicks away from accessing it.

- **Via Web Browser:**
  - Open a browser and go to stream.microsoft.com.
  - Sign in using your Microsoft 365 credentials.
- **Via Microsoft Teams:**
  - Open Teams and navigate to a channel.
  - Add Stream as a tab for easy access to video content within your team.
- **Mobile App:**
  - Download the Microsoft Stream mobile app from your app store for on-the-go video management and playback.

Pro Tip: Pin Microsoft Stream to your app launcher for quick access.

Example: Sarah logged into Stream through her web browser and added it as a tab in her team's Teams channel, ensuring her videos were just a click away.

Step 2: Uploading Your First Video

Once you've accessed Stream, it's time to upload your first video.

1. Click Create in the top menu and select Upload Video.

2. Drag and drop your video file into the upload area or browse your device to select it.

3. Add a title, description, and tags to make your video easy to find.

Pro Tip: Use descriptive titles and keywords to improve searchability within your organization.

Example: Sarah uploaded a training video titled "Introduction to Company Policies" and added tags like "HR," "Onboarding," and "Training" to ensure it was easily discoverable.

Step 3: Organizing Your Videos with Channels

Channels are a great way to group related videos and keep your content organized.

1. Click Create and select Channel.

2. Name your channel based on its purpose, such as "Team Training" or "Product Launch Resources."

3. Add videos to your channel by selecting them from your library.

Pro Tip: Create a clear naming convention for your channels to avoid confusion as your video library grows.

Example: Sarah created a channel called "HR Onboarding Videos" to centralize all content related to new employee training.

Step 4: Sharing Videos

Microsoft Stream makes it easy to share videos securely within your organization.

1. Select the video you want to share.

2. Click Share and choose your sharing preferences:

    o **Specific People:** Share with individuals or groups.

    o **Channels or Teams:** Share directly to a Stream channel or Teams channel.

    o **Embed Link:** Generate a link to embed the video in SharePoint or other platforms.

Pro Tip: Use Teams to share videos with real-time collaboration and discussion.

Example: Sarah shared her training videos with new hires by embedding them in a SharePoint onboarding site, making the resources easy to access.

Step 5: Enhancing Videos with Interactive Features

Stream allows you to make your videos more engaging with interactive features:

- **Add Captions:** Upload or generate captions to make videos accessible.

- **Enable Comments:** Encourage viewers to leave feedback or ask questions directly on the video.

- **Use Analytics:** Monitor engagement to see how your audience interacts with your videos.

Pro Tip: Add closed captions to all videos to improve accessibility and make content searchable by spoken words.

Example: Sarah added captions to her training videos, ensuring they were inclusive for team members who preferred to read along.

Step 6: Leveraging Integration with Microsoft 365

Stream's seamless integration with Microsoft 365 tools ensures your video workflow is efficient and cohesive:

- **Teams:** Save meeting recordings directly to Stream for easy sharing.
- **SharePoint:** Embed videos on pages for training, updates, or announcements.
- **OneDrive:** Store and link videos to Stream without duplicating files.
- **PowerPoint:** Insert videos into presentations to enhance storytelling.

Pro Tip: Use Power Automate to create workflows, like notifying team members when a new video is uploaded to a channel.

Example: Sarah integrated Stream with Teams, enabling her team to watch recorded meetings and collaborate on action items without switching platforms.

Step 7: Experiment and Explore

Stream's intuitive interface makes it easy to experiment with features and find what works best for your needs.

- **Try AI-Powered Search:** Use keywords to locate specific moments in videos.
- **Explore Channels:** Organize content in different ways to test what resonates with your audience.
- **Create Playlists:** Group videos into playlists for easy viewing.

Pro Tip: Encourage team members to explore Stream and share feedback on how to optimize its use.

Now that you've uploaded your first video, organized your content, and started sharing with your team, you're ready to dive deeper into Microsoft Stream's capabilities.

BEST PRACTICES FOR MICROSOFT STREAM

Microsoft Stream is more than just a video storage platform; it's a dynamic tool designed to transform the way you manage, share, and engage with video content. But like any tool, its effectiveness depends on how you use it. Adopting best practices ensures that your Stream experience is efficient, organized, and impactful.

In this chapter, we'll explore strategies to optimize your use of Stream, from organizing your content effectively to enhancing viewer engagement and leveraging its integrations with other Microsoft 365 tools.

1. Organize Content with Clear Naming Conventions

Why It Matters:
A well-organized video library makes it easier for users to find and access the content they need.

Best Practices:

- Use descriptive, consistent names for videos and channels.
- Include dates, project names, or departments in video titles.
- Group videos by theme or purpose using channels or playlists.

Example: Sarah named her onboarding videos "2024 Onboarding: Company Overview" and "2024 Onboarding: HR Policies," making them easy to identify at a glance.

Pro Tip: Establish a naming convention for your organization and share it with your team to ensure consistency.

2. Optimize Videos for Searchability

Why It Matters:
Stream's powerful search functionality can only deliver results if your videos are tagged and described effectively.

Best Practices:

- Add detailed descriptions and relevant tags to each video.

- Use keywords in video titles and descriptions to enhance discoverability.

- Enable closed captions to make spoken words searchable.

Example: Sarah added tags like "training," "onboarding," and "compliance" to her HR videos, ensuring they appeared in search results for relevant queries.

Pro Tip: Think about how users might search for your videos and include those terms in your metadata.

3. Use Interactive Features to Engage Viewers

Why It Matters:
Interactive videos hold viewers' attention longer and encourage participation.

Best Practices:

- Enable comments to foster discussion and feedback.

- Add closed captions to make videos accessible to a wider audience.

- Incorporate quizzes or polls to reinforce learning and gather insights.

Example: Sarah included a short quiz at the end of her compliance training video, helping her team retain key information while tracking participation.

Pro Tip: Regularly review comments to address questions or suggestions and keep the discussion active.

4. Leverage Analytics for Continuous Improvement

Why It Matters:
Understanding how your audience interacts with videos can help you refine your content strategy.

Best Practices:

- Monitor view counts, engagement rates, and drop-off points.
- Identify which videos perform best and replicate their structure or style.
- Use analytics to track training completion rates or assess the effectiveness of communication campaigns.

Example: Sarah noticed that videos under 10 minutes had higher completion rates, so she began breaking longer content into shorter, focused segments.

Pro Tip: Share analytics with your team to encourage collaborative improvement of video content.

5. Maintain Security and Permissions

Why It Matters:
Sensitive or proprietary content must be protected to ensure it's only accessible to the right people.

Best Practices:

- Set appropriate permissions for each video or channel, restricting access to individuals or groups as needed.
- Review permissions regularly to ensure they remain up-to-date.
- Use Stream's organization-wide settings to establish default privacy levels.

Example: Sarah restricted access to her leadership team's strategy session recordings, ensuring confidential information remained secure.

Pro Tip: Use Microsoft 365 groups to streamline permissions management for recurring audiences.

6. Integrate Stream with Other Microsoft 365 Tools

Why It Matters:
Stream is most effective when used alongside other Microsoft 365 tools, creating a seamless workflow.

Best Practices:

- Save Teams meeting recordings directly to Stream for easy sharing.

- Embed Stream videos in SharePoint pages for centralized resources.

- Add Stream tabs to Teams channels for quick access to relevant content.

- Use PowerPoint to embed Stream videos in presentations for impactful storytelling.

Example: Sarah embedded product training videos in her team's SharePoint site, ensuring her team had easy access to critical resources.

Pro Tip: Explore Power Automate workflows to notify team members when new videos are added to a Stream channel.

7. Regularly Review and Update Content

Why It Matters:
Outdated content can confuse viewers or diminish trust in your resources.

Best Practices:

- Schedule periodic reviews to ensure videos remain relevant and accurate.
- Update descriptions, tags, and metadata as necessary.
- Archive or delete obsolete content to declutter your library.

Example: Sarah reviewed her onboarding videos annually, updating policies and adding new training modules as her company evolved.

Pro Tip: Use Stream's analytics to identify videos with low engagement and decide whether to update or retire them.

8. Encourage Team Collaboration

Why It Matters:
Stream is a collaborative tool, and involving your team ensures better content and broader adoption.

Best Practices:
- Assign video creation tasks to team members based on their expertise.
- Use comments and reactions to encourage feedback and discussion.
- Share insights from analytics to involve the team in improving content.

Example: Sarah's team contributed by uploading department-specific videos to shared channels, creating a diverse and comprehensive video library.

Pro Tip: Host a team meeting to brainstorm new video ideas and encourage participation in content creation.

By adopting these best practices, you'll ensure that Microsoft Stream not only meets but exceeds your expectations. Stream has the potential to revolutionize how your organization communicates, learns, and collaborates.

TIPS AND TRICKS FOR MICROSOFT STREAM

Microsoft Stream is packed with features that can elevate your video management experience, but knowing how to unlock its hidden potential is key. From saving time to engaging your audience more effectively, these tips and tricks will help you make the most of Stream's capabilities.

Whether you're new to Stream or an experienced user, these practical insights will help you work smarter and get even more value from the platform.

1. Use AI-Powered Search to Save Time

The Trick: Stream's AI-powered search feature allows you to locate specific moments in videos by searching for spoken words, captions, or keywords.

How to Use It:

- Add captions to your videos to make them searchable.
- Use the search bar in Stream to enter a keyword or phrase.

Pro Tip: Include important keywords in your video titles and descriptions to make them more discoverable.

Example: Sarah quickly found the segment of a training video where the speaker discussed compliance policies by searching for the phrase "compliance policies."

2. Create Playlists for a Seamless Viewing Experience

The Trick: Group related videos into playlists to guide viewers through a logical sequence of content.

How to Use It:

- Create a new channel in Stream to group videos by theme or project.

- Order videos within the channel to create a flow, like an onboarding series or a product training program.

Pro Tip: Share playlists as a single link to simplify access for your audience.

Example: Sarah created a playlist for new hires, including videos on company culture, HR policies, and role-specific training.

3. Use Power Automate to Streamline Workflows

The Trick: Automate repetitive tasks like sending notifications or organizing videos with Power Automate.

How to Use It:

- Set up a flow to notify team members when a new video is uploaded to a specific channel.

- Automate video categorization by linking metadata from OneDrive to Stream.

Pro Tip: Combine Power Automate with Teams to create workflows that notify groups when training materials are updated.

Example: Sarah used Power Automate to automatically notify her team when a new compliance training video was uploaded.

4. Add Interactive Elements to Videos

The Trick: Enhance viewer engagement by adding polls, quizzes, or links to related resources in your videos.

How to Use It:

- Integrate Microsoft Forms to embed quizzes into Stream videos.

- Use the video description field to add links to supplementary materials.

Pro Tip: Use interactive elements to reinforce learning in training videos.

Example: Sarah added a quiz at the end of her HR training video to ensure employees understood key concepts.

5. Embed Videos Directly in Other Microsoft 365 Tools

The Trick: Use Stream's embed feature to integrate videos into SharePoint pages, Teams channels, or PowerPoint presentations.

How to Use It:

- Copy the embed code from your Stream video and paste it into the desired tool.
- Use the "Add a Tab" option in Teams to link Stream channels directly.

Pro Tip: Embed videos in SharePoint sites for a professional and centralized content hub.

Example: Sarah embedded a product demo video in her team's SharePoint site, making it easy for stakeholders to view and provide feedback.

6. Enable Closed Captions for Accessibility and Searchability

The Trick: Captions not only improve accessibility but also enhance search functionality within videos.

How to Use It:

- Upload a caption file when you upload your video.
- Use Stream's auto-captioning feature and edit the text for accuracy.

Pro Tip: Always review auto-generated captions to ensure they are clear and error-free.

Example: Sarah added captions to her training videos, ensuring they were accessible to all employees, including those with hearing impairments.

7. Use Copilot for Smarter Video Management

The Trick: Let Copilot assist with organizing, tagging, and summarizing your videos.

How to Use It:

- Ask Copilot to generate tags based on the video's content.
- Use Copilot to suggest video descriptions or create action items from meeting recordings.

Pro Tip: Be specific in your prompts to Copilot for more accurate and relevant suggestions.

Example: Sarah used Copilot to generate a summary for a long training video, helping her team quickly understand its content.

8. Organize Content with a "Completed Videos" Channel

The Trick: Keep your library tidy by moving outdated or completed videos to a dedicated channel.

How to Use It:

- Create a channel labeled "Archived Videos" or "Completed Content."
- Regularly review and move videos that are no longer in active use.

Pro Tip: Use tags to indicate the relevance of archived content, such as "Q4 2024 Training."

Example: Sarah archived older onboarding videos, ensuring her main training channel only featured the latest content.

9. Use Analytics to Refine Your Video Strategy

The Trick: Stream's analytics can reveal patterns in viewer behavior, helping you optimize your content.

How to Use It:

- Monitor metrics like watch time, drop-off points, and engagement rates.
- Use these insights to create shorter, more focused videos if engagement drops off early.

Pro Tip: Combine analytics with team feedback to identify content gaps or opportunities for improvement.

Example: Sarah noticed a drop-off rate halfway through her training videos and adjusted future content to be more concise and engaging.

10. Encourage Feedback from Your Team

The Trick: Invite viewers to share their thoughts on videos to improve content and collaboration.

How to Use It:

- Enable comments on videos and encourage constructive feedback.
- Use surveys or polls to gather input on what types of videos your team finds most useful.

Pro Tip: Host periodic team reviews of your Stream content to identify what's working and what can be improved.

Example: Sarah invited her team to leave comments on her training videos, sparking valuable discussions and suggestions for improvement.

These tips and tricks unlock the full potential of Microsoft Stream, helping you save time, engage your audience, and stay organized.

REVOLUTIONIZING VIDEO MANAGEMENT

Microsoft Stream is already a robust tool for managing and sharing video content, but with the addition of Copilot, an AI-powered assistant, it becomes even more dynamic. Copilot transforms how you interact with videos, offering intelligent suggestions, automating tasks, and enhancing engagement. From generating summaries to improving accessibility, Copilot streamlines workflows and unlocks new possibilities for video content.

In this chapter, we'll explore how Copilot enhances Microsoft Stream and provide actionable examples to help you leverage its capabilities.

Copilot is an AI assistant integrated into Microsoft Stream, designed to help you work smarter, not harder. It uses natural language processing and advanced AI algorithms to assist with tasks like:

- Summarizing video content.

- Generating captions and transcripts.

- Automating video tagging and categorization.

- Recommending related content or actions.

Copilot acts as your partner in video management, reducing manual effort and increasing efficiency.

How Copilot Can Help in Microsoft Stream

1. **Generate Summaries for Videos**

The Feature:
Copilot can analyze the content of your videos and create concise summaries, helping viewers quickly understand the main points.

How It Helps:

- Save time by generating a summary instead of watching the entire video.

- Provide context to team members who need a quick overview.

Example: Sarah uploaded a 30-minute training session on compliance policies. Copilot generated a summary that highlighted the key topics covered, making it easier for her team to decide whether they needed to watch the full video.

Pro Tip: Use summaries in video descriptions to enhance searchability and viewer engagement.

2. Create and Edit Captions Automatically

The Feature:
Copilot generates accurate captions for your videos, making them accessible and searchable.

How It Helps:
- Improve accessibility for viewers with hearing impairments.

- Enhance the user experience for non-native speakers.

- Enable keyword searches within video content.

Example: Sarah recorded a product demo and used Copilot to generate captions automatically. She then made minor edits to ensure accuracy before publishing the video.

Pro Tip: Review auto-generated captions for accuracy, especially for technical terms or industry-specific jargon.

3. Automate Video Tagging and Categorization

The Feature:
Copilot suggests tags and categories based on the video's content, saving you the effort of manual tagging.

How It Helps:

- Improve discoverability within your organization.
- Keep your video library organized and easy to navigate.

Example: When Sarah uploaded a series of onboarding videos, Copilot automatically tagged them with relevant keywords like "onboarding," "HR," and "new hires," ensuring they were easy to find.

Pro Tip: Combine Copilot's tags with your organization's naming conventions for maximum clarity.

4. **Identify Key Moments in Videos**

The Feature:
Copilot highlights significant moments in your videos, such as speaker transitions, key discussions, or visual changes.

How It Helps:

- Quickly locate important sections without scrubbing through the entire video.
- Provide shortcuts to specific topics for your audience.

Example: During a recorded brainstorming session, Copilot identified when each team member presented their ideas, allowing Sarah to jump to the relevant sections with ease.

Pro Tip: Use these key moments to create timestamps in your video descriptions.

5. **Recommend Related Content or Actions**

The Feature:
Based on the video's content, Copilot suggests related videos, documents, or next steps to enhance the viewer's experience.

How It Helps:

- Keep viewers engaged by directing them to additional resources.
- Build comprehensive learning paths or project workflows.

Example: After Sarah's compliance training video, Copilot recommended a related video on workplace ethics and provided a link to the company's compliance policy document.

Pro Tip: Use Copilot's recommendations to guide viewers through a curated journey, like an onboarding process or learning module.

6. **Assist with Transcripts for Meetings and Webinars**

The Feature:
When Teams meeting recordings are saved to Stream, Copilot generates detailed transcripts for easy reference.

How It Helps:
- Create searchable meeting notes for participants.
- Ensure absent team members can catch up on discussions.

Example: After a quarterly planning meeting, Sarah used Copilot to generate a transcript, which she shared with her team to ensure alignment on action items.

Pro Tip: Highlight action points in the transcript to make follow-ups more efficient.

Best Practices for Using Copilot in Microsoft Stream

1. **Be Specific with Prompts:**
   o The more detailed your request, the better Copilot can tailor its suggestions.
   o For example, instead of "Summarize this video," try "Summarize the key takeaways from the compliance training session."

2. **Combine AI and Human Insight:**

   o Review and refine Copilot's outputs to ensure they align with your needs.

   o Use Copilot's recommendations as a starting point and personalize them for your audience.

3. **Encourage Team Adoption:**

   o Train your team on how to use Copilot effectively to maximize its benefits.

   o Share examples of how Copilot has streamlined your workflow to inspire others.

Copilot is more than just a feature—it's a game-changer for video management and collaboration. By automating repetitive tasks and providing intelligent insights, it frees you to focus on creating impactful content and driving engagement.

COMMON PITFALLS HOW TO AVOID THEM

While Microsoft Stream is a powerful tool for video management, collaboration, and sharing, missteps in its use can limit its effectiveness. From poorly organized content to underutilizing key features, these common pitfalls are easily avoidable with a little foresight and planning. In this chapter, we'll explore the challenges users often encounter and provide practical advice to ensure you maximize Stream's potential.

1. Poor Organization of Video Content

The Pitfall:
Videos are scattered without a clear structure, making it difficult for team members to find relevant content.

Why It Happens:
Users may neglect to create channels or use tags and descriptions, resulting in a cluttered library.

How to Avoid It:

- Create channels based on topics, departments, or projects.

- Use consistent naming conventions for videos and channels.

- Add detailed descriptions and tags to every video.

Example: Sarah initially uploaded all her training videos without organizing them into channels, leading to confusion. By categorizing videos into "Onboarding," "Compliance Training," and "Leadership Development," she made the library intuitive and easy to navigate.

Pro Tip: Periodically review and reorganize your video library to ensure it remains user-friendly as content grows.

2. Underutilizing Search and Tagging Features

The Pitfall:
Users struggle to locate specific videos because they fail to leverage Stream's AI-powered search and tagging capabilities.

Why It Happens:
Tags and metadata are overlooked during the upload process.

How to Avoid It:

- Add relevant tags and keywords to each video.
- Use Stream's AI-powered transcription to make spoken words searchable.
- Train team members to use the search bar effectively.

Example: Sarah started tagging her videos with terms like "HR Training" and "2024 Onboarding" to make them easier to find. She also used captions to ensure key phrases were searchable.

Pro Tip: Include commonly used terms in your organization as tags to align with how team members search for content.

3. Ignoring Accessibility Features

The Pitfall:
Videos lack captions or transcripts, making them inaccessible to some team members.

Why It Happens:
Users may not be aware of Stream's accessibility tools or underestimate their importance.

How to Avoid It:

- Enable auto-captioning and review for accuracy.
- Provide transcripts for meeting recordings and training videos.
- Use accessible design principles when creating video content.

Example: Sarah enabled captions for her compliance videos, ensuring team members with hearing impairments could fully engage with the content.

Pro Tip: Treat captions and transcripts as essential, not optional, for all video content.

4. Failing to Manage Permissions Properly

The Pitfall:
Sensitive videos are either too restricted, causing access issues, or too open, risking data security.

Why It Happens:
Permissions are set hastily or left at default settings.

How to Avoid It:

- Assign permissions based on the intended audience for each video or channel.

- Regularly review and update permissions to reflect changes in team roles or projects.

- Use organization-wide settings to establish default privacy rules.

Example: Sarah accidentally left a leadership strategy video open to all employees, causing a minor security concern. She quickly adjusted the permissions to limit access to the management team.

Pro Tip: Use Microsoft 365 groups to simplify permission management for recurring audiences.

5. Overloading Videos with Lengthy Content

The Pitfall:
Videos are too long, leading to decreased viewer engagement and retention.

Why It Happens:
Users try to cover too much in a single video instead of breaking it into smaller segments.

How to Avoid It:

- Keep videos concise, ideally under 10 minutes.
- Divide lengthy content into shorter, focused videos or create playlists.
- Use Copilot to summarize longer videos for easier navigation.

Example: Sarah noticed low engagement on her 30-minute onboarding video. By splitting it into three shorter segments, she significantly increased viewership and completion rates.

Pro Tip: Use analytics to identify where viewers drop off and adjust future videos accordingly.

6. Neglecting Analytics

The Pitfall:
Users don't track video performance, missing opportunities to improve content.

Why It Happens:
Analytics are underutilized or misunderstood.

How to Avoid It:

- Regularly review view counts, engagement metrics, and drop-off points.
- Use insights to refine video length, style, or content focus.
- Share analytics with your team to encourage collaborative improvement.

Example: Sarah used analytics to discover that her compliance videos were most often watched in the mornings, prompting her to schedule training sessions at that time for maximum engagement.

Pro Tip: Track trends over time to identify consistent patterns and adapt your strategy.

7. Overlooking Integration Opportunities

The Pitfall:
Stream is used in isolation, missing the benefits of integration with other Microsoft 365 tools.

Why It Happens:
Users may not know how to connect Stream with Teams, SharePoint, or OneDrive.

How to Avoid It:

- Save Teams meeting recordings directly to Stream for easy access.
- Embed Stream videos in SharePoint pages for centralized resources.
- Link OneDrive videos to Stream for broader sharing.

Example: Sarah embedded her training videos into a SharePoint site, creating a one-stop resource hub for new employees.

Pro Tip: Explore Power Automate workflows to connect Stream with other tools and automate repetitive tasks.

8. Relying Too Heavily on Manual Processes

The Pitfall:
Manual tagging, categorizing, and sharing can be time-consuming and prone to errors.

Why It Happens:
Users may not utilize Copilot or automation features to their full potential.

How to Avoid It:

- Use Copilot to generate tags, captions, and summaries.

- Automate workflows with Power Automate for repetitive tasks.

- Train your team to use AI features effectively.

Example: Sarah saved hours by using Copilot to generate summaries for her training videos, enabling her to focus on higher-level tasks.

Pro Tip: Experiment with Copilot prompts to discover its full range of capabilities.

By avoiding these common pitfalls, you'll ensure your experience with Microsoft Stream is smooth, efficient, and impactful.

SARAH'S JOURNEY WITH MICROSOFT STREAM

The morning sunlight streamed through the office windows as Sarah stared at her inbox, overwhelmed by a flood of emails. As the company's training coordinator, she had just wrapped up a week of onboarding sessions for new hires, but the process had been anything but smooth. Her biggest challenge? Managing an ever-growing library of training videos scattered across different platforms, emails, and hard drives.

"Sarah, can you resend the compliance training video? I can't find the link," one email read.

"Can we make the leadership session recording easier to access for the team?" another asked.

Sarah sighed. There had to be a better way.

Later that day, during a team meeting, her colleague James shared a recent success he'd had with Microsoft Stream. "It's a game-changer," he said, showing how he'd organized his department's video library into searchable channels and even added captions to improve accessibility.

Intrigued, Sarah decided to give Stream a try. She logged in through her Microsoft 365 account, and within minutes, she was greeted by an intuitive interface that seemed built to solve her problems.

Sarah started by uploading the compliance training video that her HR department relied on for onboarding. Stream guided her to add a title, description, and relevant tags like "training," "HR," and "compliance." She then created a channel called "Onboarding Essentials" and grouped related videos, including the company overview and benefits walkthrough.

For the first time, Sarah could see her training content neatly organized in one place. "This might actually work," she thought, feeling a glimmer of hope.

Sarah's next challenge was making the videos more engaging. She discovered Stream's interactive features and decided to enable comments on her videos. This simple addition allowed new hires to ask questions directly within the training videos, fostering real-time discussions.

She also experimented with captions, using Copilot to auto-generate text. After a quick review to ensure accuracy, the captions were ready. Not only did this make the videos more accessible, but it also allowed users to search for specific terms within the videos.

During the next onboarding session, Sarah encouraged employees to watch the videos at their own pace, ask questions in the comments, and revisit key sections using the search function. The response was overwhelmingly positive.

One evening, Sarah realized she'd forgotten to summarize the leadership training video she had just uploaded. Instead of panicking, she turned to Copilot. With a single prompt—"Summarize the key takeaways from this video"—Copilot generated a concise, clear summary in seconds.

"Why haven't I been using this all along?" Sarah thought.

She also used Copilot to generate tags for her older videos, saving her hours of manual work. With suggestions like "strategy," "team building," and "goal setting," the videos became far easier to organize and find.

The real magic happened when Sarah integrated Stream with the rest of Microsoft 365. She embedded training videos into her team's SharePoint site, creating a centralized hub for all onboarding materials. She also added Stream tabs to her department's Teams channels, making it simple for team members to access recordings of past meetings and brainstorming sessions.

By using Power Automate, Sarah even set up a notification workflow that alerted team members whenever a new video was added to the onboarding channel. These integrations turned Stream into the backbone of her team's video strategy.

Of course, Sarah encountered a few hiccups along the way. Initially, she had uploaded several videos without organizing them into channels, which caused confusion. But after reviewing best practices, she quickly adjusted, grouping videos logically and adding consistent naming conventions.

She also realized that some of her videos were too long and engagement dropped off halfway through. To address this, she began breaking them into shorter, more focused segments.

By the time the next onboarding cycle rolled around, Sarah felt prepared. She kicked off the program by sharing a link to the "Onboarding Essentials" channel, which housed all the training materials new hires would need.

The feedback was immediate and enthusiastic. "The videos were so easy to find and follow," one new hire said. Another commented, "I loved being able to pause, rewind, and search for specific topics."

Sarah knew she had achieved something meaningful. Stream had not only simplified her workflow but also improved the training experience for everyone involved.

Sarah's story illustrates the transformative power of Microsoft Stream. From organizing scattered videos to creating an engaging and accessible experience, Stream turned Sarah's overwhelming workload into a streamlined success.

Like Sarah, you can use Stream to overcome video management challenges, enhance collaboration, and foster a more connected and productive environment.

LESSONS FROM MICROSOFT STREAM

As we wrap up this exploration of Microsoft Stream, let's reflect on the transformative journey we've taken—from understanding its core features to discovering its full potential through real-world applications. Along the way, Sarah's story offered a relatable and inspiring example of how Stream can simplify video management, enhance engagement, and foster collaboration.

This chapter revisits the key lessons from the book while reflecting on Sarah's journey and how it mirrors the experiences of many users stepping into the world of Stream.

1. **What Is Microsoft Stream?**
   Stream is more than a video platform; it's a comprehensive tool for creating, managing, and sharing video content. Its seamless integration with Microsoft 365 tools like Teams, SharePoint, and OneDrive makes it a central hub for all your video needs.

2. **Why Use Microsoft Stream?**
   Stream helps you centralize video content, improve accessibility, and boost engagement through interactive features like comments, captions, and analytics. It's not just about storing videos—it's about unlocking their full potential.

3. **Getting Started with Stream:**
   Starting with Stream is easy, whether you're uploading your first video, organizing content into channels, or sharing videos securely. Its intuitive interface and integration capabilities make it accessible to users of all skill levels.

4. **Best Practices and Tips:**
   From using clear naming conventions to leveraging analytics and AI features, best practices ensure you get the most out of Stream. Tips like automating workflows with Power Automate or

embedding videos in SharePoint sites make your processes even more efficient.

5. **The Role of Copilot:**
   Copilot's AI-powered assistance enhances video management by generating summaries, captions, and tags, and by helping you organize content quickly and intelligently.

6. **Common Pitfalls:**
   By avoiding issues like poor organization, underutilized features, and improper permissions, you can make Stream a seamless part of your workflow.

7. **Sarah's Journey:**
   Through Sarah's story, we saw how Stream transformed her chaotic video library into a streamlined, collaborative resource hub. Her experience illustrates the practical application of everything you've learned in this book.

Sarah's transformation from feeling overwhelmed to confident reflects the journey many users experience when they first adopt Microsoft Stream. Her story is a testament to the power of persistence, curiosity, and the right tools.

Sarah's initial challenges—scattered videos, accessibility issues, and lack of engagement—are common hurdles. But by embracing Stream's features and best practices, she turned these challenges into opportunities:

- **Centralization:** By organizing her videos into channels, Sarah made her content easy to find and navigate.

- **Engagement:** Interactive features like comments and captions brought her training sessions to life, fostering better communication and learning.

- **Efficiency:** Copilot's assistance saved Sarah time, allowing her to focus on higher-value tasks.

Her journey mirrors that of readers like you who are looking to improve their video strategies. Just as Sarah discovered the value of Stream step by step, you too can unlock its potential by applying the lessons from this book to your own projects.

Microsoft Stream is a tool for transformation—both for your workflow and your organization's approach to video. As you integrate Stream into your daily tasks, remember that learning is an ongoing process. Experiment with its features, embrace its integrations, and explore how it can work alongside other Microsoft 365 tools.

The power of Stream lies in its versatility. Whether you're managing training videos, hosting virtual events, or collaborating on team projects, it adapts to your needs and scales with your ambitions.

Sarah's journey doesn't end here, and neither does yours. As you continue to refine your use of Stream, consider exploring the other tools in the Microsoft 365 ecosystem to enhance your productivity even further. From Teams to SharePoint, OneDrive to Power Automate, each tool complements the other, creating a unified experience.

EXPANDING YOUR JOURNEY WITH MICROSOFT STREAM

As we conclude this book, it's clear that Microsoft Stream is more than just a tool for video storage—it's a transformative platform that empowers individuals and organizations to communicate, collaborate, and learn more effectively. From the first step of uploading a video to leveraging advanced features like Copilot, Stream offers a wealth of possibilities to enhance your workflow and engagement.

But this is just the beginning. Microsoft Stream is part of the broader Microsoft 365 ecosystem, and its true power lies in how seamlessly it integrates with tools like Teams, SharePoint, OneDrive, and Power Automate. By mastering Stream, you've taken a significant step toward unlocking the full potential of this interconnected suite of tools.

Stream doesn't operate in isolation. Its real value shines when it's used as part of a larger strategy to improve communication, collaboration, and productivity across your organization. Here's how Stream fits into the Microsoft 365 ecosystem:

- **With Teams:** Record meetings and share recordings instantly, keeping your team aligned and informed.

- **With SharePoint:** Create centralized hubs for video content, ensuring resources are easy to find and access.

- **With OneDrive:** Store videos securely and link them to Stream for broader sharing.

- **With Power Automate:** Automate repetitive tasks like notifications and video tagging, saving time and reducing errors.

By integrating these tools, you can create a seamless, unified workflow that amplifies your impact.

Sarah's story reminds us that growth and learning are ongoing processes. Just as she started with small steps—uploading a single video, organizing her content, and experimenting with Copilot—you too can build on what you've learned here to achieve even greater success.

Every new video you create, every workflow you streamline, and every audience you engage represents an opportunity to grow. The lessons from this book are designed to empower you to use Stream not just as a tool, but as a catalyst for transformation.

Technology is constantly evolving, and staying ahead means embracing a mindset of continuous learning. Microsoft Stream, like the rest of the Microsoft 365 suite, will continue to grow with new features and integrations that offer even more ways to enhance your work.

This book is part of the *Microsoft 365 Companion Series*, and there are many other resources available to help you explore the full range of tools at your disposal. Whether you're diving into Teams, SharePoint, or OneDrive, each tool has unique strengths that complement Stream and create endless possibilities for innovation.

Thank you for joining us on this journey through Microsoft Stream. The skills and strategies you've gained here are just the beginning of what's possible. With creativity, curiosity, and a commitment to learning, you can continue to expand your capabilities and achieve new heights in your professional and personal endeavors.

Your next step? Explore how Stream integrates with the other tools in Microsoft 365, and continue building a workflow that empowers you and your team to work smarter, communicate better, and achieve more.

Here's to your success with Microsoft Stream—and beyond!

www.ingramcontent.com/pod-product-compliance
Lightning Source LLC
Chambersburg PA
CBHW071032050326
40689CB00014B/3623